I0413123

Molecular Population Genetic Structure in the Piping Plover

By Mark P. Miller and Susan M. Haig, U.S. Geological Survey, Cheri L. Gratto-Trevor, Environment Canada, Thomas D. Mullins, U.S. Geological Survey

Open-File Report 2009–1032

U.S. Department of the Interior
U.S. Geological Survey

U.S. Department of the Interior
KEN SALAZAR, Secretary

U.S. Geological Survey
Suzette Kimball, Acting Director

U.S. Geological Survey, Reston, Virginia: 2009

For more information on the USGS—the Federal source for science about the Earth, its natural and living resources, natural hazards, and the environment, visit http://www.usgs.gov or call 1-888-ASK-USGS. For an overview of USGS information products, including maps, imagery, and publications, visit *http://www.usgs.gov/pubprod*

To order this and other USGS information products, visit *http://store.usgs.gov*

Suggested citation: Miller, M.P., Haig, S.M., Gratto-Trevor, C.L., and T.D. Mullins, 2009, Molecular population genetic structure in the Piping Plover: U.S. Geological Survey Open-File Report 2009-1032, 30 p.

Contents

Figures

Tables

Conversion Factors

Multiply	By	To obtain
Volume		
microLiter (µL)	3.4×10^{-5}	fluid ounces

Temperature in degrees Celsius (°C) may be converted to degrees Fahrenheit (°F) as follows: $°F=(1.8 \times °C)+32$.

Abbreviations

milliMolar (mM)
microMolar (µM)
nanogram (ng)
Units (U)
Molecular Weight (MW)

Molecular Population Genetic Structure in the Piping Plover

By Mark P. Miller and Susan M. Haig, U.S. Geological Survey, Cheri L. Gratto-Trevor, Environment Canada, Thomas D. Mullins, U.S. Geological Survey

Executive Summary

The Piping Plover (*Charadrius melodus*) is a migratory shorebird currently listed as Endangered in Canada and the U.S. Great Lakes, and threatened throughout the remainder of its U.S. breeding and winter range. In this study, we undertook the first comprehensive molecular genetic-based investigation of Piping Plovers. Our primary goals were to (1) address higher level subspecific taxonomic issues, (2) characterize population genetic structure, and (3) make inferences regarding past bottlenecks or population expansions that have occurred within this species. Our analyses included samples of individuals from 23 U.S. States and Canadian Provinces, and were based on mitochondrial DNA sequences (580 bp, n = 245 individuals) and eight nuclear microsatellite loci (n = 229 individuals). Our findings illustrate strong support for separate Atlantic and Interior Piping Plover subspecies (*C. m. melodus* and *C. m. circumcinctus*, respectively). Birds from the Great Lakes region were allied with the Interior subspecies group and should be taxonomically referred to as *C. m. circumcinctus*. Population genetic analyses suggested that genetic structure was stronger among Atlantic birds relative to the Interior group. This pattern indicates that natal and breeding site fidelity may be reduced among Interior birds. Furthermore, analyses suggested that Interior birds have previously experienced genetic bottlenecks, whereas no evidence for such patterns existed among the Atlantic subspecies. Likewise, genetic analyses indicated that the Great Lakes region has experienced a population expansion. This finding may be interpreted as population growth following a previous bottleneck event. No genetic evidence for population expansions was found for Atlantic, Prairie Canada, or U.S. Northern Great Plains individuals. We interpret our population history insights in light of 25 years of Piping Plover census data. Overall, differences observed between Interior and Atlantic birds may reflect differences in spatiotemporal stability of Piping Plover nesting habitat between regions.

Introduction

The Piping Plover (*Charadrius melodus*) has long been a species of conservation concern throughout its range (fig. 1). In Canada, two subspecies of Piping Plover are recognized: *C. m. melodus* in the Atlantic Canada region and *C. m. circumcinctus* in Ontario and Prairie Canada. Both subspecies are listed as endangered under the Species at Risk Act (Department of Justice Canada, 2002; Committee on the Status of Endangered Wildlife in Canada, 2003). Pursuant to the U.S. Endangered Species Act, the Piping Plover is listed as endangered in the Great Lakes watershed and threatened in the rest of its breeding and winter range (U.S. Fish and Wildlife Service, 1985). The U.S. Fish and Wildlife Service has approved separate recovery plans for populations breeding on the Atlantic Coast (U.S. Fish and Wildlife Service, 1988a, 1996), Great Lakes (U.S. Fish and Wildlife Service, 2003), and Northern Great

Plains (U.S. Fish and Wildlife Service, 1988b). Primary threats include nest and chick disturbance stemming from habitat degradation associated with human land use and development practices. Predation also has been suggested as a pertinent threat (Cuthbert and Roche, 2008). Complete species censuses over the past 25 years have documented range expansions, contractions, and local extirpations as well as areas where numbers have increased or decreased (Haig and Oring, 1985; Haig and Plissner, 1993; Plissner and Haig, 2000; Haig and others, 2005; Elliott-Smith and Haig, 2009).

Despite continued conservation concerns, there has not been a modern molecular genetic study carried out to address higher level taxonomic issues or elucidate population patterns and processes. A primary topic of need is a formal evaluation of subspecific taxonomic status, where two distinct subspecies are currently recognized: *C. m. melodus* are thought to breed in the Atlantic North America whereas *C. m. circumcinctus* have been described as Interior breeders (American Ornithologists' Union, 1957; Elliott-Smith and Haig, 2004). Subspecific identification of Great Lakes birds has not been resolved, although an early allozyme study described them as belonging to the Interior subspecies (Haig and Oring, 1988a). From a recovery perspective, clarifying Piping Plover taxonomic issues may be important for informing listing and status reviews, establishing management strategies, and prioritizing funding under the U.S. Endangered Species Act and the Canadian Species at Risk Act.

Understanding taxonomy and population structure on multiple geographic and temporal scales provides critical details into a species' status and changes in status that is almost impossible to carry out without taking a molecular approach. The genetic affinity of populations is routinely used to determine the degree of vulnerability of species at risk or of population segments within species. Thus, in this study, we used mitochondrial DNA (mtDNA) sequence analyses to examine taxonomic issues and provide a historic perspective on population structure in Piping Plovers. For comparison, we also developed and analyzed variable microsatellite markers to provide a more recent assessment of population structure issues in Piping Plovers. Our analyses focused on two separate hierarchical levels. As a primary level, we separately quantified patterns within Interior and Atlantic birds (that is, putative subspecies). This partitioning of individuals was later substantiated by data generated in this study (see sections "Results" and "Discussion"). Subsequent analyses also were performed where the data were further subdivided to reflect samples from Prairie Canada, U.S. Great Plains, Great Lakes, Atlantic Canada, and Atlantic United States (table 1). Although likely not pertinent from an organismal perspective, the latter hierarchical level reflected geographical regions encompassed by separate U.S. and Canadian recovery plans that have been outlined for Piping Plovers, and therefore provide a basis for informing resource managers regarding species status in their local area of charge. Taken together, these analyses provide a comprehensive assessment of population genetics for the species and serve as a basis for comparison with other measures of population status such as censuses and other demographic parameters.

Methods

Sample Collection

Following protocols outlined by the American Ornithologists' Union (Gaunt and Oring, 1997), blood or tissue samples were collected from breeding populations throughout the Piping Plover North American breeding range (fig. 1). No known close relatives (for example, parent/offspring, siblings, etc.) were included in analyses and all samples were collected during the breeding season prior to immigration of birds from other sites. Collection dates for birds included in our study are provided in appendix 1.

Laboratory Methods

Mitochondrial DNA

Due to a problematic poly-C 5' region in the control region, internal primers PPL26L (CCCCATACTAAATTCTTAGTATGTTTGC) and PPL657 (CACGGACGAAAATGATGATATATAGC) were designed to generate an approximately 650bp bi-directional DNA sequence in domains I and II of the control region. Amplifications were performed using a PTC 100 thermal cycler (MJ Research). A total reaction volume of 20 μL was used with the following concentrations: 10 mM Tris-HCl at pH 8.3; 50 mM KCl; 0.001% gelatin; 3.5 mM $MgCl_2$; 100 μM for each of the dNTPs; 0.2 μM of each primer; 100 ng of template; and 1.5 U AmpliTaq Gold Polymerase (Perkin Elmer). The following parameters were used for amplifications: 12 min. denaturation at 93°C, followed by 35 cycles of 30 sec. at 93°C, annealing at 50°C for 30 sec., and elongation at 72°C for 1 min. A final 10 min. period of elongation at 72°C followed the last cycle. Successful PCR reactions were cleaned and concentrated by centrifugation dialysis using Microcon 30,000 MW cutoff filters (Amicon Bioseparations). Bidirectional DNA sequence was generated in domains I and II of the control region with flanking primers PPL26L and PPL657 and internal primers TS437L (Wenink and others, 1994) and PPL493H (GGTCTTGAAGCTAGTAACGTAGGA). Sequences were generated using ABI Prism Big Dye Terminator Cycle Sequencing chemistry on an ABI 3100 capillary DNA automated sequencer (377 DNA Sequencer ABI Prism 377XL Collection Software) located in the Central Services Laboratory at Oregon State University. Ambiguities were resolved by comparing light and heavy-strand sequences or from overlap of different fragments. The final sequence alignment contained 580bp of data from 245 individuals sampled at 23 U.S. States and Canadian Provinces (table 1, fig. 1).

Microsatellites

Microsatellite primer sequences were obtained from a number of sources. Primers CALEX-8, 13, 35, and 37 (developed for Kentish Plovers, *C. alexandrinus*) were obtained from the Sheffield Molecular Genetic Facilities, University of Bath, UK (Küpper and others, 2007). Microsatellite locus C201 was obtained from ISSR-suppression-PCR clone libraries (Lian and others, 2001; Funk and others, 2007), and microsatellite markers PPL4, 10, and 11 were isolated using a magnetic bead capture enrichment protocol (Glenn and Schable, 2005).

Sample screening amplifications were performed using a PTC 100 thermal cycler (MJ Research). A total reaction volume of 10 μL was used with the following concentrations: 10 mM Tris-HCl at pH 8.3; 50 mM KCl; 0.001% gelatin; 3.5 mM $MgCl_2$; 100 μM for each of the dNTPs; 0.2 μm of each primer; 100 ng of template; and 1.5 U GoTaq DNA polymerase (Promega). The following parameters were used for amplifications: 3 min. denaturation at 93°C, followed by 35 cycles of 30 sec. at 93°C, annealing at 52 - 62°C for 30 sec., and elongation at 72°C for 1 min. A final 10 min. period of elongation at 72°C followed the last cycle. Amplification products were analyzed on an ABI 3100 capillary DNA automated sequencer located in the Central Services Laboratory at Oregon State University. ABI Genescan® analysis software was used to size fragments based on internal lane standard GeneScan 500 [Rox]. ABI Genotyper® software was used to score alleles sizes. The final microsatellite data set contained genotypes from 229 individuals sampled from 23 U.S. States and Canadian Provinces (table 1, fig. 1).

Data Analyses

Genetic Diversity Patterns

The computer program Arlequin 3.1 (Excoffier and others, 2005) was used to quantify genetic diversity measures for each geographic region within our hierarchy. Gene and nucleotide diversity values were obtained for mitochondrial sequence data whereas observed and expected heterozygosity values (H_O and H_E, respectively) were calculated for microsatellite data. At the secondary level, tests for deviations from Hardy-Weinberg genotypic proportions were performed using GDA version 1.1 (Lewis and Zaykin, 2002).

Phylogenetic Analysis

Four independent approaches were used to characterize phylogenetic relationships among the observed mitochondrial haplotypes. First, Arlequin was used to generate a minimum spanning tree. Second, computer programs TCS (Clement and others, 2000) and NETWORK (http://www.fluxus-engineering.com) were used to generate statistical parsimony and median-joining networks, respectively. Finally, the program MultiPhyl Online (Keane and others, 2007) was used to generate phylogenies based on the maximum likelihood (ML) criterion. For the latter analysis, an appropriate model of DNA sequence evolution was identified using the program ModelGenerator (Keane and others, 2006) with the AIC2 model selection measure and four discrete Gamma categories. The tree search was implemented using the nearest neighbor interchange algorithm and was initialized with a simple neighbor-joining tree.

Genetic Structure

Patterns of genetic structure were analyzed and quantified in several different ways. Data were analyzed using the AMOVA procedure as implemented in Arlequin. In these analyses, Φ_{ST} and F_{ST} was calculated (for mitochondrial and microsatellite data, respectively) to quantify the overall degree of differentiation between: (1) Interior and Atlantic groups, and (2) overall degree of differentiation among the five geographical regions corresponding to our secondary hierarchical structure. Pairwise values of Φ_{ST} and F_{ST} also were obtained for each combination of the five regions examined. Significance tests for all statistics were obtained using a randomization procedure based on 10,000 randomization replicates. *P*-values derived from pairwise tests were evaluated using sequential Bonferroni corrections. To facilitate interpretation of the pairwise comparisons, matrices of Φ_{ST} and F_{ST} values were further analyzed using MEGA4 (Tamura and others, 2007) to generate neighbor-joining trees illustrating general patterns of dissimilarity among the five regions.

Spatial genetic structure patterns were analyzed via spatial autocorrelation analyses (Sokal and Oden, 1978a, 1978b) using the computer program Alleles in Space (Miller, 2005) to determine if isolation-by-distance patterns existed within each dataset. Analyses were performed separately for the mitochondrial and microsatellite data, and independent analyses were likewise performed for the Interior and Atlantic regions. Ten thousand randomization replicates were used to identify sets of spatial distances over which significantly large or small average inter-individual genetic distance patterns occurred. Analyses were performed using 20 distance classes. Analysis results were interpreted using the general guideline of Epperson (2005), who suggested that inferences from spatial autocorrelation analyses are most concrete when the shortest distance class demonstrates significant deviations from random expectations.

The Bayesian clustering procedure implemented in computer program STRUCTURE version 2.2.3 (Pritchard and others, 2000) was used to simultaneously infer the number of distinct genetic clusters suggested by the microsatellite data, and likewise probabilistically assign each analyzed individual to one of the inferred clusters. STRUCTURE analyses were performed using values of K (the assumed number of clusters) ranging from 1 to 8. Analyses were performed using an initial burn-in of $2*10^6$ steps, followed by $1.5*10^7$ Markov-Chain Monte Carlo (MCMC) analysis sweeps. Default analysis options including assumption of an admixture model and correlated allele frequencies were used, as suggested by the authors (Falush and others, 2003). Ten replicate analyses were performed using each value of K. Values of K that produced the highest average likelihood scores over replicates were summarized and visualized using the computer programs CLUMPP version 1.1.1 (Jakobsson and Rosenberg, 2007) and DISTRUCT version 1.1 (Rosenberg, 2004), respectively.

Population History and Status

Both datasets were used to evaluate population status with respect to changes in population size and the presence of past bottleneck events. Analyses were performed at the highest hierarchical level (using Interior and Atlantic birds separately), as well as for each of the five geographical regions defined for the secondary hierarchical level. For the mitochondrial sequence data, we tested for evidence of a population expansion using mismatch distributions (Rogers and Harpending, 1992; Schneider and Excoffier, 1999), Tajima's (1989a, 1989b) D, Fu's (1997) F_S, and the R2 statistic of Ramos-Onsins and Rozas (2002). Tests using mismatch distributions, D, and F_S were performed using Arlequin, and P-values were estimated based on comparison of observed values with expectations derived from 10,000 coalescent-based simulations. The R2 test and its significance were calculated and tested as described above using the computer program DnaSP version 4.5 (Rozas and others, 2003). Note that mismatch distribution tests use a null hypothesis of a population expansion, whereas the other analyses explicitly use a stable population as a null hypothesis.

Microsatellite data were used to test for recent bottlenecks at each of the hierarchical levels described above using the computer program BOTTLENECK (Cornuet and Luikart, 1996). Given the low allelic richness and narrow size ranges of observed microsatellite alleles (see section "Results"), analyses were performed separately using a strict stepwise-mutational model (SMM) and with the two-phase model (TPM) based on a TPM variance of 4 (corresponding to an average of an approximately two-step repeat motif change when non-stepwise changes occur; DiRienzo and others, 1994) and an assumed proportion of 70 percent fixed SMM events. Ten thousand simulation replicates were used in analyses. Excess heterozygosity relative to theoretical expectations, an indication of past bottlenecks, was evaluated using the Wilcoxon signed-rank test.

Results

Genetic Diversity Patterns

In our analyses of mitochondrial sequence variation, 70 unique haplotypes were observed among the 245 total individuals analyzed in this study (table 2). Twenty-five unique haplotypes were observed among the 96 Interior birds examined, whereas 49 haplotypes were identified among 149 Atlantic individuals. Only four haplotypes were shared between Interior and Atlantic groups. Among Interior birds, gene diversity and nucleotide diversity corresponded to 0.813 and 0.0030, respectively (table 3). Corresponding values were higher for Atlantic birds (gene diversity: 0.917, nucleotide diversity: 0.0051). Among the five geographical regions described by the secondary hierarchical structure, genetic diversity was highest within the Atlantic U.S. group (gene diversity: 0.961, nucleotide diversity: 0.0056) and lowest within the Great Lakes region (gene diversity: 0.596, nucleotide diversity: 0.0020) (table 3).

Microsatellite markers revealed slightly different trends (table 3). At the highest hierarchical level, H_O and H_E were higher for the Interior (H_O: 0.3930, H_E: 0.3990) group relative to the Atlantic group (H_O: 0.2461, H_E: 0.2509). Among the five geographical regions, diversity was highest for Prairie Canada samples (H_O: 0.4063, H_E: 0.4098) and lowest for the Atlantic Canada group (H_O: 0.2308, H_E: 0.2211). The microsatellite data were generally characterized by relatively low allelic richness (table 3). Among 40 tests for deviation from Hardy-Weinberg genotypic proportions, four significant results at the $\alpha = 0.05$ level were observed: three from the Prairie Canada group (loci Calex8, Calex37, and Calex35) and one from the U.S. Great Plains group (locus Calex37). With the exception of locus Calex8, all significant tests suggested heterozygote deficiencies. Within the Prairie Canada group, Calex8 displayed a slight but significant excess of heterozygotes (that is, nominally consistent with a population bottleneck).

Phylogenetic Analysis

All four phylogeny reconstruction procedures produced similar results. For simplicity, we present only the ML and minimum spanning trees (figs. 2-3). With respect to the ML tree, ModelGenerator identified the TrN+I+G model as the correct model of nucleotide substitution (nucleotide frequencies: A = 0.259, C = 0.300, G = 0.147, T = 0.295; Gamma parameter = 0.38; proportion of invariant sites = 0.84). The final tree had a likelihood score of -1299.091. The primary pattern revealed by phylogenetic analyses was the strong differentiation between Interior and Atlantic birds. Aside from four shared haplotypes observed between Interior and Atlantic individuals (haplotypes 1, 2, 18, and 25), the remaining phylogenetic diversity was well-partitioned into clearly separable groups (table 2; figs. 2-3). Five of the six haplotypes observed within birds sampled from the Great Lakes region were strongly allied with other haplotypes observed within Interior birds (table 2; haplotypes 1, 13, 15, 23, 24). The sixth haplotype observed among Great Lakes birds (haplotype 25), although shared with a few Atlantic individuals, was nonetheless relatively closely related to other Interior haplotypes (figs. 2-3).

Genetic Structure

All analyses suggested the presence of strong genetic structure. In comparisons of Atlantic versus Interior birds, Φ_{ST} and F_{ST} (for mitochondrial and microsatellite data, respectively) corresponded to 0.473 and 0.104 ($P < 0.0001$). Likewise, Φ_{ST} and F_{ST} values generated when analyzing data using five regional groups corresponded to 0.426 ($P < 0.0001$) and 0.098 ($P < 0.0001$), respectively. Furthermore, similar patterns were observed between nuclear and mitochondrial marker data sets when comparing all pairwise values of Φ_{ST} and F_{ST} (fig. 4). In general, pairwise genetic differentiation values were smaller for contrasts within either the Interior or Atlantic groups relative to between-group contrasts. Genetic distances among Interior regions were also smaller than the genetic distance between the Atlantic Canada and Atlantic U.S. regions. However, within the Interior region, significant F_{ST} values were nonetheless observed for contrasts between Prairie Canada and the U.S. Great Plains and for contrasts between the Great Lakes and U.S. Great Plains (fig. 4). Consistent with phylogenetic analyses, neighbor-joining trees generated from each matrix indicated that birds from the Great Lakes region were allied with those from the Interior region (fig. 4).

Spatial autocorrelation analyses gave different results for the Atlantic versus Interior regions (fig. 5). Among Atlantic birds, analyses indicated that significant spatial genetic structure existed in mitochondrial and microsatellite datasets. Although genetic structure patterns were stronger for the mitochondrial data, both datasets revealed patterns where individuals from the smallest distance class displayed pairwise genetic distance values that were significantly smaller than random expectations (figs. 5A, 5B). In contrast, analyses of Interior birds revealed no such patterns, as the average genetic distances of individuals from the smallest distance class were non-significant (figs. 5C, 5D). Interior birds revealed highly variable patterns where significantly large or small values generally were observed inconsistently among distance classes in a manner that did not reflect an overall isolation-by-distance pattern.

Consistent with other analyses, STRUCTURE suggested that the most likely partitioning of the data exists for the $K = 2$ case (fig. 6A). When visualized, proportions of individual genomes assigned to each cluster generally suggested that the two clusters corresponded to separate Interior and Atlantic groups (fig. 6B). Likewise, and consistent with phylogenetic analyses, individuals from the Great Lakes region (Michigan and Wisconsin) were primarily assigned to the cluster associated with Interior birds.

Population History and Status

With one exception, insights obtained from mitochondrial data were inconsistent across the four separate analysis types performed (table 4). Mismatch distribution analyses and Fu's F_S statistic generally tended to suggest evidence of population expansions, whereas Tajima's D and the R2 statistic suggested population stability. The primary exception to this pattern was the Great Lakes region, where all four analyses provided evidence for an expanding population. Tests for the signature of past population bottleneck events (microsatellite data), in contrast, provided relatively clear statistical patterns. All analyses performed on Interior birds and the three separate partitions of those data detected bottlenecks (table 4). In contrast, no evidence for bottleneck events was identified among Atlantic individuals.

Discussion

Subspecies Status

Our combined analyses of mitochondrial DNA sequence data and eight nuclear microsatellite loci provided numerous insights into the taxonomic status of Piping Plover subspecies, and likewise provided information regarding genetic structure and historical patterns within different hierarchical units. With respect to subspecific taxonomic patterns, previous allozyme-based genetic data (Haig and Oring, 1988a) were unable to provide support for the presence of separate Interior and Atlantic subspecies that had been proposed based on the geographical distribution of breast-band patterns (Moser, 1942; American Ornithologists' Union, 1945). However, our use of more modern and variable genetic information systems and analyses of a substantially larger data set than Haig and Oring (1988a) illustrated strong differentiation between Interior and Atlantic birds (table 2, figs. 2, 3, 4, and 6). This pattern is highly consistent with prior field-based observations that suggested little migration of individuals between regions (Haig and Oring, 1988b), and consequently, provides strong evidence in support of separate Atlantic and Interior subspecies (*C. melodus melodus* and *C. m. circumcinctus*, respectively; American Ornithologists' Union, 1957). Among 70 unique haplotypes detected (table 2), only four (5.3 percent) were shared between what were otherwise monophyletic groups. Furthermore, if we assume that "Atlantic" haplotypes are those that were observed solely or in the majority among Atlantic individuals (with the complement being true for "Interior haplotypes" and Interior birds), then 93 percent of the Atlantic birds differ from 99 percent of Interior birds (table 5). This pattern exceeds the well-known "75 percent rule" for defining subspecies (Amadon, 1949; Patten and Unitt, 2002; Haig and others, 2006). Likewise, given the large Φ_{ST} and F_{ST} values observed between Interior and Atlantic groups (fig. 4), our data also meet the subspecies definition of Funk and others (2007), who defined a subspecies as "… a subset of populations with consistent genetic differences from other subsets of populations at multiple independent loci, with genetic differences consisting of significant variation in microsatellite allele and mtDNA haplotype frequencies, the presence of unique alleles or haplotypes, and significant net sequence divergence." Our data also illustrated that birds from the Great Lakes region are strongly allied with the Interior group, and should be taxonomically referred to as *C. m. circumcinctus*. Note that genetic evidence for two Piping Plover subspecies contrasts with weak genetic differentiation among U.S. Snowy Plovers (*C. alexandrinus*; Funk and others, 2007). Given the strong patterns of differentiation observed between *C. m. melodus* and *C. m. circumcinctus*, we suggest that future research evaluating adaptive divergence or reproductive isolation of subspecies may be informative.

Regional Genetic Structure

Differential genetic structure patterns were observed within subspecies. Within the Interior group (Prairie Canada, U.S. Great Plains, Great Lakes), pairwise Φ_{ST} and F_{ST} values (for mitochondrial and microsatellite data, respectively) were markedly lower than comparable values generated for contrasts between Atlantic Canada and the Atlantic U.S. (fig. 4). This pattern may reflect higher individual gene flow (reduced breeding site fidelity) of Interior birds relative to birds from the Atlantic region. However, despite producing lower pairwise values, significant F_{ST} values were nonetheless observed in the Interior region for two of the three pairwise contrasts (fig. 4). This result suggests that the Interior subspecies does not represent a single panmictic entity. Field observations appear to corroborate this idea, as over 20 years of bird banding studies have never identified Great Lakes birds breeding west of Lake Superior (or vice versa) (J. Dingledine, USFWS, and F. Cuthbert, University of Minnesota, personal communication). Consequently, long-distance gene flow, when it occurs, may be episodic and insufficient to maintain demographic connectivity of regions.

Spatial genetic structure patterns (fig. 5) were also in agreement with pairwise Φ_{ST} and F_{ST} values, as Atlantic birds show evidence of isolation-by-distance patterns. In this case, our data suggest that dispersal, when it occurs, generally is associated with movement to relatively proximal breeding territories. In contrast, Interior birds showed no overt spatial genetic structure signals. This pattern is consistent with the reduced genetic differentiation among Interior subregions (fig. 4), and may reflect reduced breeding site or natal fidelity when previously occupied sites are unavailable because they are flooded, dry, overgrown with vegetation, or otherwise disturbed due to human activities. Overall, differences observed between Interior and Atlantic birds may reflect variation in habitat stability between regions. Atlantic regions may provide more reliable, long-term habitat for Piping Plovers that is less likely to demonstrate extreme spatiotemporal variability. In contrast, the Interior region of North America experiences substantial temporal climatic variation that may cause flooding or complete desiccation of alkali lakes and other wetlands in an area (Espie and others, 1998; Haig and others, 2005). Further, anthropogenically controlled variable water/flooding regimes on the Missouri River may periodically force dispersal of many birds nesting in the Great Plains if habitat becomes unavailable due to inundation, vegetation encroachment, or other habitat disturbances (North, 1986; Schwalback and others, 1993, as cited in Espie and others, 1998).

Genetic Diversity, Population Status, and History

Piping Plover genetic diversity appeared to be comparable to the range of values observed in two Snowy Plover subspecies sampled from the continental U.S. and Caribbean (Funk and others, 2007).

Snowy Plovers also are a species of conservation concern although only one Distinct Population Segment is ESA-listed for the species (U.S. Fish and Wildlife Service, 1993). For example, mitochondrial control region nucleotide diversity in our five regions (table 3) ranged from 0.0020 to 0.0056 (mean = 0.0044) compared with a range of 0.0006 to 0.0083 at the same locus in Snowy Plovers (mean = 0.0042). Average expected microsatellite heterozygosity within each region (table 3; range: 0.2211-0.4098, mean = 0.3334) likewise fell within the range of values observed for Snowy Plovers (range = 0.249 - 0.539, mean = 0.453). The slightly higher average value observed for Snowy Plovers likely reflects differences in allelic richness of the microsatellite loci investigated in this study and by Funk and others (2007). Among eight microsatellite loci examined here, numbers of alleles ranged from 2 to 5 (mean = 2.875) across our full dataset. In contrast, an average of 4.8 alleles per locus (range = 2 to 10) were present among the 10 loci examined by Funk and others (2007).

Consistent with our phylogenetic and genetic structure analyses, our evaluations of population status and history suggested differences between Interior versus Atlantic Piping Plovers (table 4). For example, microsatellite analyses indicated that each of the three Interior subregions (and all Interior birds combined) show evidence of past genetic bottleneck events, whereas no such patterns were observed among Atlantic birds. Note that tests based on the stepwise mutational model (SMM) tend to be highly conservative relative to those based on the two-phase model (TPM) (Cornuet and Luikart, 1996). Consequently, given the significance of both SMM and TPM-based analyses, our data provide compelling evidence for past bottlenecks within the Interior region. In contrast, tests for population expansions based on the mitochondrial sequence data provided inconsistent results among analysis variants and geographical regions (table 4), with the two most powerful tests (F_S and R2; Fu, 1997, Ramos-Onsins and Rozas, 2002) generally providing conflicting results. Of all analyses performed, only the Great Lakes subregion illustrated consistent evidence for an expanding population (table 4).

The timing and intensity of influential historical events can be difficult to infer based solely on genetic data. For example, detection of bottlenecks depends on the interplay of a multivariate combination of statistical and population parameters that primarily include: (1) size of the pre-bottleneck population, (2) size of the post-bottleneck population, (3) duration of the bottleneck event, (4) number of sampled individuals for analyses, and (5) number of loci examined (Cornuet and Luikart, 1996; Luikart and others, 1998). Likewise, the power of tests for population expansions primarily depend on: (1) expansion rate, (2) elapsed time since the expansion event, (3) sample size, and (4) degree of variability among the set of observed sequences (Fu, 1997; Ramos-Onsins and Rosas, 2002).

Historical records and prior census data (Haig and Oring, 1985; Haig and Plissner, 1993; Plissner and Haig, 2000; Haig and others, 2005; Elliott-Smith and Haig, 2009), however, tend to corroborate the general inferences provided by our analyses. For example, in the mid-1980s, less than 2000 Piping Plover breeding pairs were estimated to exist in North America (Haig and Oring, 1985), with only approximately 17 pairs inhabiting the Great Lakes region (U.S. Fish and Wildlife Service, 1985; Haig and Oring, 1988b). These estimates are thought to reflect severe population declines that began in the early 1900s (Haig and Oring, 1985, 1988b), and are likely to be the basis for our detection of significant bottleneck events among Interior birds. However, available data do not allow us to provide more explicit temporal estimates, nor do they allow us to determine if the same (or different) bottleneck events influenced all Interior regions. Furthermore, data from four International censuses over 15 years suggest that population increases have occurred in the Great Lakes region. Between 1991 and 2006, the number of birds counted in the Great Lakes during censuses increased by 175 percent (from 40 to 110 birds; Haig and Plissner, 1993; Elliott-Smith and Haig, 2009). This increase is likely due to intense predator management and habitat protection (Wemmer, 2000). Consequently, our data may be illustrating the genetic repercussions of a population expansion and recovery process that followed a prior bottleneck event among Great Lake birds. In contrast, Prairie Canada and the U.S. Great Plains only show consistent evidence for a prior bottleneck: no evidence for population expansions was obtained from the genetic data. This finding also is consistent with census data, which suggests that increases in Prairie Canada and the U.S. Great Plains have been modest (3,467 birds in 1991 compared to 4,662 in 2006; Haig and Plissner, 1993; Elliott-Smith and Haig, 2009). Though apparently on a positive growth trajectory, these other regions may not be increasing at sufficient rates to facilitate population expansion detection by genetic data. Alternately, given the relatively recent collection dates of the birds analyzed (appendix 1), more time may be required for the molecular genetic signal of the recent expansions to become manifest.

In contrast to Interior birds, Atlantic populations illustrated no evidence of genetic bottlenecks or population expansions. If our hypothesis regarding the relative stability of Atlantic versus Interior habitats is correct (see section "Regional Genetic Structure"), then Atlantic birds may not have experienced historical population reductions or bottlenecks of the magnitude seen by Interior birds. Furthermore, census data (Haig and Plissner; 1993; Elliott-Smith and Haig, 2009) indicate that the Atlantic Canada population has changed little from 1991 to 2006 (513 birds in 1991 and 457 in 2006), suggesting relatively stable current population sizes. Moreover, although the Atlantic U.S. population appears to have almost doubled in size (1,462 birds were observed in 1991 and 2,855 in 2006), the overall census size within the region was always relatively large. For example, when comparing smallest census numbers, the Atlantic U.S. population has been more than 20 times larger than the Great Lakes population (Haig and Plissner, 1993; Elliott-Smith and Haig, 2009). Also, although the overall Atlantic U.S. population is currently increasing, it has decreased in some local areas. Thus, the molecular genetic signal of the expansion may not yet be detectable within the genealogy of Piping Plovers from the region. Absence of a consistent signal (table 4) may reflect an initially diverse population prior to expansion, result from inclusion of samples from locations where sub-regional declines have been noted, or indicate that the rate of population growth (relative to the initial population size) is insufficient to allow for detection of the current expansion event.

Conclusions

Results of our research (1) provide molecular genetics-based confirmation for the existence of two distinct Piping Plover subspecies (*C. m. melodus* and *C. m. circumcinctus*), (2) suggest that Atlantic populations are more stable than their Interior counterparts, and (3) provide evidence that Interior birds have undergone recent population bottlenecks. Our detection of significant signals of a population expansion among Great Lakes birds is highly consistent with International Piping Plover census data.

Acknowledgments

We thank the USGS Forest and Rangeland Ecosystem Science Center and Canadian Wildlife Service STAGE effort for funding this study. We are further thankful for discussions and comments regarding this report from Elise Elliott-Smith (USGS, FRESC) and Anne Hecht (U.S. Fish and Wildlife Service). Many people have contributed invaluable samples to this project and we are deeply grateful for their assistance: Irv Ailes, Diane Amirault, Sebastian Brennan, Sue Canale, Jeff Cordes, Francie Cuthbert. Jennifer Dare, Brian Dirks, Nick Dufef, Jackie Fung, N. Gibbons, Keith Gordon, Robert Gough, Amy Joa, Kevin Johnson, Casey Kruse, Marcia Lyons, Jean McArthur, Scott McBurney, E. McMichaels, Allison Nichols, Greg Pavelka, Ray Perez, Sue Philhower, Rob Powell, Noah Olenych, Andrew Orgonik, Patrick Railey, Shanna Ramsey, Claude Roy, Francios Shaffer, John Sidle, Jennifer Stucker, Griff Venaton, Gordon Warrick, SallieWelte, and Theresa Zadi.

References Cited

Amadon, D., 1949, The seventy-five percent rule for subspecies: Condor, v. 51, p. 250-258.

American Ornithologists' Union, (1945), Twentieth supplement to the check-list of North American birds: The Auk, v. 62, p. 436–449.

American Ornithologists' Union, 1957, Check-list of North American Birds, 5th ed: Union, Washington, D.C., Am. Ornithol.

Clement, M., Posada, D., and Crandall, K., 2000, TCS: a computer program to estimate gene genealogies: Molecular Ecology, v. 9, p. 1657-1660.

Committee on the Status of Endangered Species in Canada, 2003, Canadian species at risk, May 2003: Ottawa, Ontario, Committee on the Status of Endangered Species in Canada.

Cornuet, J.M., and Luikart, G., 1996, Description and power analysis of two tests for detecting recent population bottlenecks from allele frequency data: Genetics, v. 144, p. 2001-2014.

Cuthbert, F.J., and Roche, E.A., 2008, The Piping Plover in Michigan: a 100 year perspective: Michigan Birds and Natural History, v. 15, p. 29-38.

Department of Justice Canada, 2002, Annual Statutes of Canada 2002, Chapter 29, Species at Risk Act, Schedule 1, Part 2.

DiRienzo, A.C., Peterson, A.C., Garza, J.C., Valdes, A.M., Slatkin, M., and Freimer, N.B., 1994, Mutational processes of simple-sequence repeat loci in human populations: Proceedings of the National Academy of Sciences, USA, v. 91, p. 3166-3170.

Elliott-Smith, E., and Haig, S.M., 2004, Piping Plover (*Charadrius melodus*), *in* Poole, A., ed., The Birds of North America Online, Ithaca: Cornell Lab of Ornithology: Birds of North America website at http://bna.birds.cornell.edu/bna/species/002.

Elliott-Smith, E., Haig, S.M., and Powers, B.M., 2009, Data from the 2006 International Piping Plover Census: U.S. Geological Survey Data Series 426, 332 p.

Epperson, B.K., 2005, Estimating dispersal from short distance spatial autocorrelation: Heredity, v. 95, p. 7-15.

Espie, R.H.M., James, P.C., and Brigham R.M., 1998, The effects of flooding on Piping Plover *Charadrius melodus* reproductive success at Lake Diefenbaker, Saskatchewan, Canada: Biological Conservation. v. 86, p. 215-222.

Excoffier, L., Laval, G., and Schneider, S., 2005, Arlequin ver. 3.0: An integrated software package for population genetics data analysis: Evolutionary Bioinformatics Online, v. 1, p. 47-50.

Falush, D., Stephens, M., and Pritchard, J.K., 2003, Inference of population structure: Extensions to linked loci and correlated allele frequencies: Genetics, v. 164, p. 1567-1587.

Fu, Y.-X., 1997, Statistical tests of neutrality of mutations against population growth, hitchhiking and background selection: Genetics, v. 147, p. 915-925.

Funk, W.C., Mullins, T.D., and Haig, S.M., 2007, Conservation genetics of the Snowy Plovers (*Charadrius alexandrinus*) in the Western Hemisphere: population genetic structure and delineation of subspecies: Conservation Genetics, v. 8, p. 1287-1309.

Gaunt, A.S., and Oring, L.W., 1997, Guidelines to the Use of Wild Birds in Research: Washington, D.C., The Ornithological Council.

Glenn, T.C., and Schable, N.A., 2005, Isolating microsatellite DNA loci: Methods in Enzymology, v. 395, p. 202-222.

Haig, S.M., and Oring, L.W., 1985, Distribution and status of the Piping Plover throughout the annual cycle: Journal of Field Ornithology, v. 56, p. 334-345.

Haig, S.M., and Oring, L.W., 1988a, Genetic differentiation of Piping Plovers across North America: The Auk, v. 105, p. 260-267.

Haig, S.M., and Oring, L.W., 1988b, Distribution and dispersal in the Piping Plover: The Auk, v. 105, p. 630–638.

Haig, S.M., Ferland, C.L., Cuthbert, F.J., Dingledine, J., Goossen, J.P., Hecht, A., and McPhillips, N., 2005, A complete species census and evidence for regional declines in Piping Plovers: Journal of Wildlife Management, v. 69, p. 160-173.

Haig, S.M., and Plissner, J.H., 1993, Distribution and abundance of Piping Plovers: Results and implications of the 1991 international census: Condor , v. 95, p. 145-156.

Haig, S.M., Beever, E.A., Chambers, S.M., Draheim, H.M., Dugger, B.G., Dunham, S., Elliott-Smith, E., Fontaine, J.B., Kessler, D.C., Knaus, B.J., Lopes, I.F., Loschl, P., Mullins, T.D., and Sheffield, L.M., 2006, Taxonomic considerations in listing subspecies under the U.S. Endangered Species Act: Conservation Biology, v. 20, p. 1584-1594.

Jakobsson, M., and Rosenberg, N.A., 2007, CLUMPP: A cluster matching and permutation program for dealing with label switching and multimodality in analysis of population structure: Bioinformatics, v. 23, p. 1801-1806.

Keane, T.M., Creevey, C.J., Pentony, M.M., Naughton, T.J., and McInerney, J.O., 2006, Assessment of methods for amino acid matrix selection and their use on empirical data shows that ad hoc assumptions for choice of matrix are not justified: BMC Evolutionary Biology, v. 6, p. 29.

Keane, T.M., Naughton, T.J., and McInerney, J.O., 2007, MultiPhyl: A high-throughput phylogenomics webserver using distributed computing: Nucleic Acids Research, v. 35, p. W33-W37.

Küpper, C., Horsburgh, G.J., Dawson, D.A., French-Constant, R., Szekely, T., and Burke, T., 2007, Characterization of 36 polymorphic microsatellite loci in the Kentish plover (*Charadrius alexandrinus*) including two sex-linked loci and their amplification in four other Charadrius species: Molecular Ecology Notes, v. 7, p. 35-39.

Lewis, P., and Zaykin, D., 2002, GDA: Genetic Data Analysis, Computer software distributed by authors from http://hydrodictyon.eeb.uconn.edu/people/plewis/software.php.

Lian, C., Zhou, Z., and Hogetsu, T., 2001, A simple method for developing microsatellite markers using amplified fragments of inter-simple sequence repeat (ISSR): Journal of Plant Research, v.114, p. 381–385.

Luikart, G., Allendorf, F.W., Cornuet, J.M., and Sherwin, W.B., 1998, Distortion of allele frequency distributions provides a test for recent population bottlenecks: Journal of Heredity, v. 89, p. 238-247.

Miller, M.P., 2005, Alleles in Space: computer software for the joint analysis of interindividual spatial and genetic structure: Journal of Heredity, v. 96, p. 722-724.

Moser, R.A., 1942, Should the Belted Piping Plover be recognized as a valid race?: Nebraska Bird Review, v. 10, p. 31–37.

North, M.R., 1986, Piping plover nest success on Mallard Island in North Dakota and implications for water level management: Prairie Naturalist, v. 18, p. 117-122.

Patten, M.A., and Unitt, P., 2002, Diagnosability versus mean differences of Sage Sparrow subspecies: The Auk, v. 119, p. 26-35.

Plissner, J.H., and Haig, S.M., 2000, Status of a broadly-distributed endangered species: results and implications of the second international Piping Plover census: Canadian Journal of Zoology, v. 78, p. 1-12.

Pritchard, J.K., Stephens, M., and Donnelly, P., 2000, Inference of population structure using multilocus genotype data: Genetics, v. 155, p. 945-959.

Ramos-Onsins, S.E., and Rozas, J., 2002, Statistical properties of new neutrality tests against population growth: Molecular Biology and Evolution, v. 19, p. 2092-2100.

Rogers, A.R., and Harpending, H., 1992, Population growth makes waves in the distribution of pairwise genetic differences: Molecular Biology and Evolution, v. 9, p. 552-569.

Rosenberg, N.A., 2004, Distruct: A program for the graphical display of population structure: Molecular Ecology Notes, v. 4, p. 137–138.

Rozas, J., Sanchez-Delbarrio, J.C., Messeguer, X., and Rozas, R., 2003, DnaSP, DNA polymorphism analyses by the coalescent and other methods: Bioinformatics, v. 19, p. 2496-2497.

Schneider, S., and Excoffier, L., 1999, Estimation of demographic parameters from the distribution of pairwise differences when the mutation rates vary among sites: Application to human mitochondrial DNA: Genetics, v. 152, p. 1079-1089.

Schwalbach, M.J., Higgins, K.F., Dinan, J., Dirks, B.J., and Kruse, C.D., 1993, Effects of water levels on interior Least Tern and Piping Plover nesting along the Missouri river in South Dakota, Pages 75-81 in: Proceedings, the Missouri River and its Tributaries: Piping Plover and Least Tern Symposium (eds. Higgins, K.F. and Brashier, M.R.), South Dakota State University, Brookings, SD.

Sokal, R.R., and Oden, N.L., 1978a, Spatial autocorrelation analysis in biology. I. Methodology: Biological Journal of the Linnaean Society, v. 10, p. 199-228.

Sokal, R.R., and Oden, N.L., 1978b, Spatial autocorrelation analysis in biology. II. Some biological implications and four applications of evolutionary and ecological interest: Biological Journal of the Linnaean Society, v. 10, p. 229-249.

Tajima, F., 1989a, Statistical method for testing the neutral mutation hypothesis by DNA polymorphism: Genetics, v. 123, p. 585-595.

Tajima, F., 1989b, The effect of change in population size on DNA polymorphism: Genetics, v. 123, p. 597-601.

Tamura, K., Dudley, J., Nei, M., and Kumar, S., 2007, MEGA4: Molecular Evolutionary Genetics Analysis (MEGA) software version 4.0. Molecular Biology and Evolution, v. 24, p. 1596-1599.

U.S. Fish and Wildlife Service, 1985, Determination of endangered and threatened status for the Piping Plover: Federal Register 50, p. 50726-50734.

U.S. Fish and Wildlife Service, 1988a, Atlantic Coast Piping Plover Recovery Plan: Newton Corner, Massachusetts, U.S. Fish and Wildlife Service.

U.S. Fish and Wildlife Service, 1988b, Great Lakes and Northern Great Plains Piping Plover Recovery Plan: Twin Cities, Minnesota, U.S. Fish and Wildlife Service.

U.S. Fish and Wildlife Service, 1993, Determination of threatened status for the Pacific Coast population of the western snowy plover: Federal Register, v. 58. p. 12864-12874.

U.S. Fish and Wildlife Service, 1996, Piping Plover (*Charadrius melodus*) Atlantic Coast Population: Revised Recovery Plan: Hadley, Massachusetts, U.S. Fish and Wildlife Service.

U.S. Fish and Wildlife Service, 2003, Recovery Plan for the Great Lakes Piping Plover (*Charadrius melodus*): Fort Snelling, Minnesota, U.S. Fish and Wildlife Service.

Wemmer, L., 2000, Conservation of the Piping Plover (*Charadrius melodus*) in the Great Lakes region: A landscape ecosystem approach: Minneapolis, Minnesota, University of Minnesota, Ph.D. dissertation.

Wenink, P.W., Baker, A.J., and Tilanus, M.G.J., 1994, Mitochondrial control-region sequences in two shorebird species, the turnstone and the dunlin, and their utility in population genetic studies: Molecular Biology and Evolution, v. 11, p. 22-31.

Table 1. Sample sizes and collection locations for genetic analyses of Piping Plovers.

Locations			Sample size (mitochondrial)	Sample size (microsatellite)
Interior			96	92
	Prairie Canada		29	27
		Alberta	7	6
		Saskatchewan	19	18
		Manitoba	3	3
	U.S. Great Plains		50	51
		Montana	4	5
		North Dakota	20	20
		South Dakota	19	20
		Nebraska	6	5
		Minnesota	1	1
	Great Lakes		17	14
		Wisconsin	1	1
		Michigan	16	13
Atlantic			149	137
	Atlantic Canada		69	67
		Quebec	20	20
		Newfoundland	2	1
		New Brunswick	6	6
		Prince Edward Island	20	20
		Nova Scotia	21	20
	Atlantic U.S.		80	70
		Maine	6	6
		Massachusetts	1	2
		Delaware	2	2
		Maryland	17	16
		Rhode Island	3	2
		New York	20	19
		New Jersey	22	17
		North Carolina	9	6
Total			245	229

Table 2. Geographical locations where 70 unique Piping Plover haplotypes were detected. Only haplotypes 1, 2, 18, and 25 were shared between Interior and Atlantic birds.

Haplotype	Prairie Canada			Northern Great Plains					Great Lakes		Atlantic Canada					Atlantic U.S.								Total
	AB	SK	MB	MT	ND	SD	NE	MN	WI	MI	QB	NF	NB	PI	NS	ME	MA	DE	MD	RI	NY	NJ	NC	
1	1	7	1	2	6	9		1	1	10			2											40
2	2	2	1		6	4				1		1		2	4									23
3	2																							2
4	1		1																					2
5	1																							1
6		3		2																				5
7		1																						1
8		1																						1
9		3																						3
10		1																						1
11		1																						1
12					1		1																	2
13							1			1														2
14					3																			3
15					2	1				1														4
16						1																		1
17						2																		2
18						1	1																1	3
19					1																			1
20					1																			1
21							1																	1
22							2																	2
23						1				1														2
24										1														1
25										1						1			3		1			6
26											11	1	3	7	9					2	2	2	1	38
27											7			4										11
28											2													2
29													1											1
30														2										2
31														1										1
32														2										2
33														1										1
34														1										1
35															1					1		4		6
36															1				1		2	3		7
37															4						2	1		7
38															1						2	1	2	6
39															1									1
40																1								1
41																1								1
42																1								1
43																1								1
44																	1							1
45																1		1						2
46																					5	5		10
47																		1						1
48																			1					1
49																			1					1
50																			2					2
51																			1					1
52																			2					2
53																					2	1		3
54																					3			3
55																			1					1
56																			1					1
57																			1					1
58																			1					1
59																			1					1
60																			1					1
61																					1			1
62																						1		1
63																						1		1
64																						1		1
65																						2		2
66																							1	1
67																							1	1
68																							1	1
69																							1	1
70																							1	1
Total	7	19	3	4	20	19	6	1	1	16	20	2	6	20	21	6	1	2	17	3	20	22	9	245

15

Table 3. Genetic diversity measures for mitochondrial and microsatellite data sets observed at two hierarchical levels for Piping Plovers.

[Na, average number of alleles per locus; H_O, observed heterozygosity; H_E, expected heterozygosity]

Region	Mitochondrial			Microsatellite		
	Number of haplotypes	Gene diversity	Nucleotide diversity	Na	H_O	H_E
Interior	25	0.813	0.0030	2.500	0.3930	0.3990
Atlantic	49	0.917	0.0051	2.375	0.2461	0.2508
Subregion						
Prairie Canada	11	0.867	0.0039	2.500	0.4063	0.4098
U.S. Great Plains	15	0.829	0.0028	2.250	0.3607	0.3857
Great Lakes	7	0.596	0.0020	2.125	0.3839	0.3882
Atlantic Canada	16	0.765	0.0032	1.875	0.2308	0.2211
Atlantic U.S.	38	0.961	0.0056	2.250	0.2417	0.2622

Table 4. Demographic analyses for Piping Plovers designed to infer the presence of population expansions (mitochondrial data) and bottleneck events (microsatellite data).

Grouping	Mitochondrial data				Microsatellite data	
	Mismatch distribution (P-value)[1]	D (P-value)[2]	Fs (P-value)[2]	R2 (P-value)[2]	SMM (P-value)[3]	TPM (P-value)[3]
All Interior	0.406	-1.5889 (0.024)	-20.3129 (<0.001)	0.0437 (0.062)	0.027	0.010
Prairie Canada	0.734	-0.6021 (0.314)	-3.6942 (0.026)	0.0993 (0.282)	0.027	0.010
U.S. Great Plains	0.278	-1.1642 (0.110)	-8.9296 (< 0.001)	0.0678 (0.113)	0.027	0.010
Great Lakes	0.932	-1.5655 (0.044)	-3.4771 (0.001)	0.0911 (0.009)	0.027	0.027
All Atlantic	0.453	-1.1343 (0.107)	-26.4361 (<0.001)	0.0526 (0.143)	0.594	0.469
Atlantic Canada	0.004	-0.2662 (0.454)	-7.5245 (0.001)	0.0931 (0.446)	0.313	0.313
Alantic U.S.	0.148	-0.9277 (0.187)	-26.3295 (<0.001)	0.0662 (0.203)	0.594	0.344

[1]H_0: Population has experienced a recent, detectable population expansion.

  Rejection of H_0 provides evidence for population stability

[2]H_0: Population has been demographically stable.

  Rejection of H_0 may reflect population expansions

[3]H_0: Population has not experienced a bottleneck

  Rejection of H_0 suggests a prior bottleneck event

Consistent with expansion
Consistent with bottleneck

Table 5. A 2 x 2 contingency table illustrating the numbers and percents of Atlantic vs. Interior birds that harbored either an "Atlantic haplotype" or "Interior haplotype". "Atlantic haplotypes" were defined as those observed solely or in the majority among Atlantic individuals (with the complement being true for "Interior haplotypes" and Interior birds).

	Atlantic Birds	Interior Birds	Total
Atlantic Haplotypes	139 (93%)	1 (1%)	140
Interior Haplotypes	10 (6%)	95 (99%)	105
Total	149	96	245

Figure 1. Collection locations of Piping Plovers analyzed in this investigation. Shaded U.S. states or Canadian provinces highlight general geographical regions. Symbols reflect specific collection locations (Circles: Interior group; Squares: Atlantic group). See table 1 for additional sample size information.

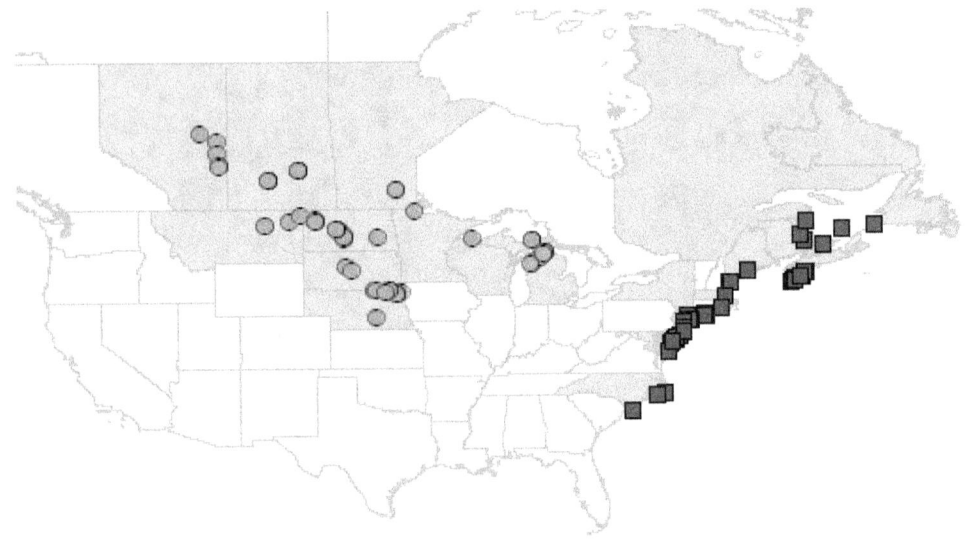

Figure 2. Minimum spanning tree illustrating relationships of 70 unique haplotypes detected among 245 Piping Plovers. Locations where haplotypes were observed are shown in table 2. Asterisks indicate four haplotypes that were shared between Interior and Atlantic birds (haplotypes 1, 2, 18, and 25).

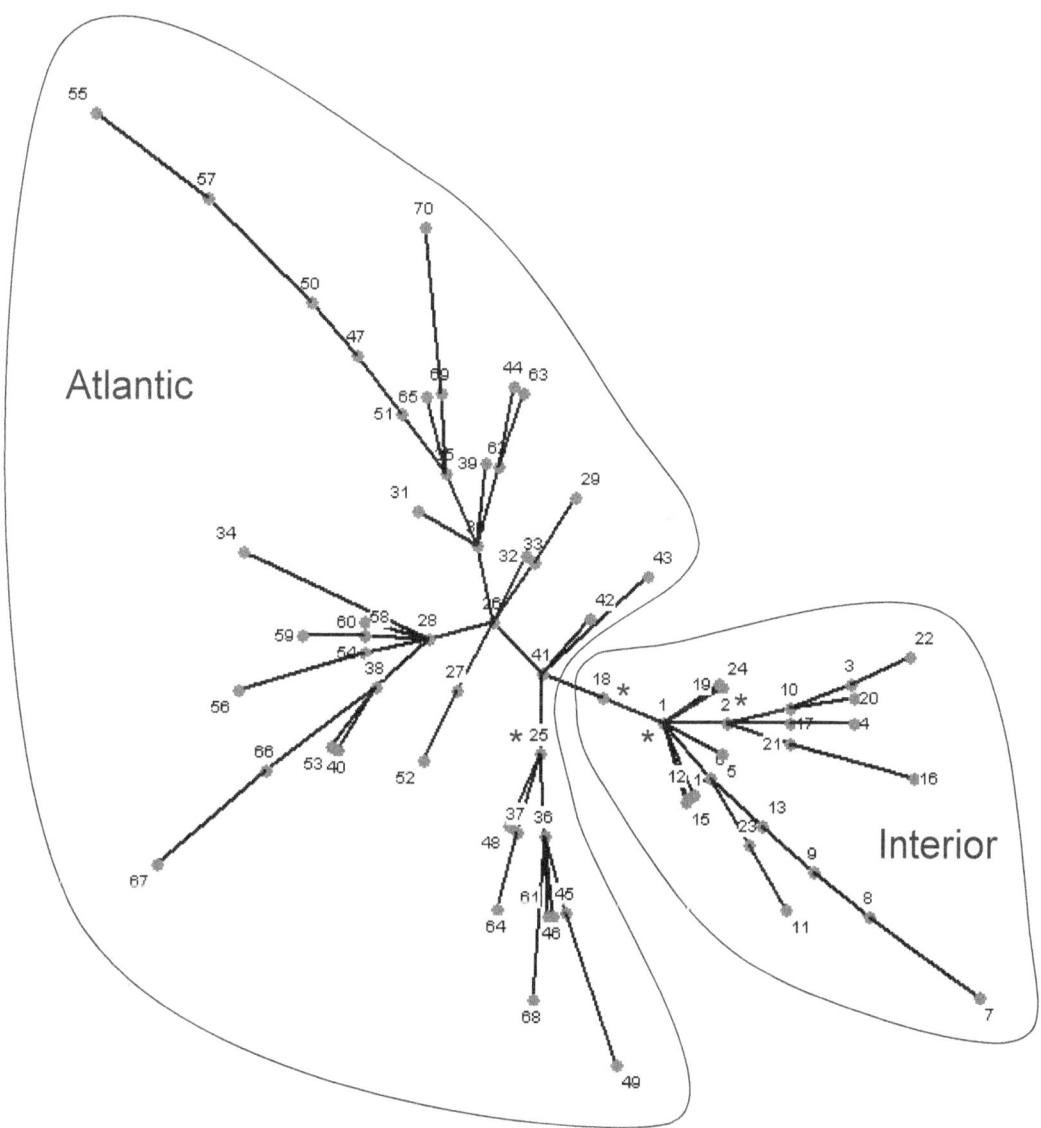

Figure 3. Maximum likelihood tree illustrating relationships of 70 unique haplotypes detected among 245 Piping Plovers. Locations where haplotypes were observed are shown in table 2. Asterisks indicate four haplotypes shared between Interior and Atlantic birds (haplotypes 1, 2, 18, and 25).

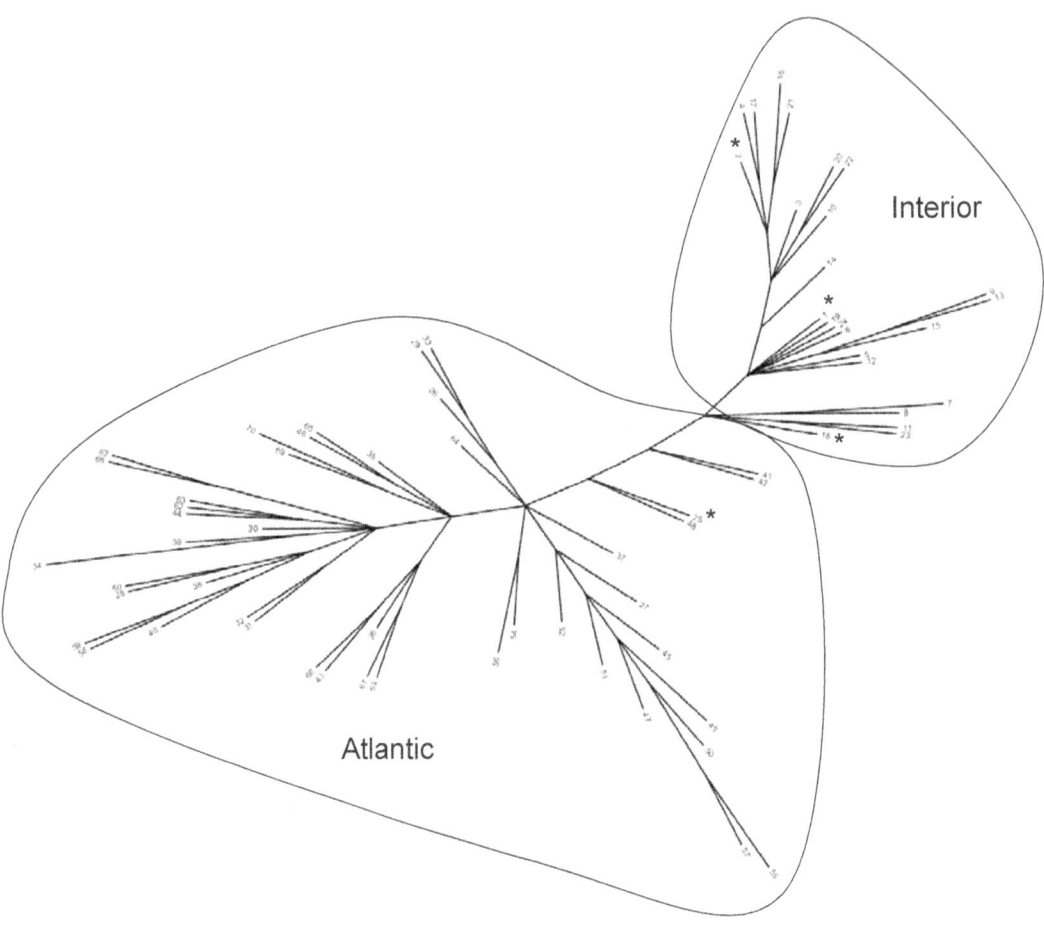

Figure 4. Pairwise Φ_{ST} (panel A) and F_{ST} (panel B) values observed from all pairwise comparisons of the five geographical regions examined for Piping Plovers. Actual statistics are contained within the lower off-diagonal elements, whereas congruent *P*-values are listed in the upper off-diagonal elements. Significant *P*-values after sequential Bonferroni correction are in bold italic type. Neighbor-joining trees to the right of each matrix illustrate relative dissimilarity of the regions based on the pairwise matrices.

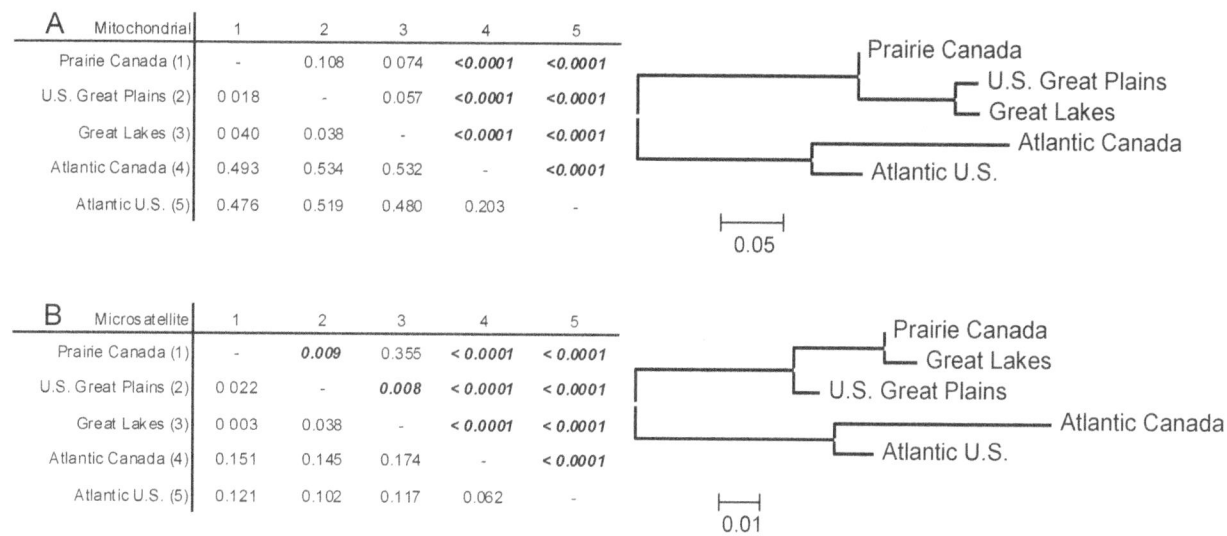

A Mitochondrial	1	2	3	4	5
Prairie Canada (1)	-	0.108	0 074	*<0.0001*	*<0.0001*
U.S. Great Plains (2)	0 018	-	0.057	*<0.0001*	*<0.0001*
Great Lakes (3)	0 040	0.038	-	*<0.0001*	*<0.0001*
Atlantic Canada (4)	0.493	0.534	0.532	-	*<0.0001*
Atlantic U.S. (5)	0.476	0.519	0.480	0.203	-

B Microsatellite	1	2	3	4	5
Prairie Canada (1)	-	*0.009*	0.355	*< 0.0001*	*< 0.0001*
U.S. Great Plains (2)	0 022	-	*0.008*	*< 0.0001*	*< 0.0001*
Great Lakes (3)	0 003	0.038	-	*< 0.0001*	*< 0.0001*
Atlantic Canada (4)	0.151	0.145	0.174	-	*< 0.0001*
Atlantic U.S. (5)	0.121	0.102	0.117	0.062	-

Figure 5. Results of spatial autocorrelation analyses based on pairwise genetic and geographical distances between individual Piping Plovers for (A) mitochondrial data generated from the Atlantic region, (B) microsatellite data generated for the Atlantic region, (C) mitochondrial data generated from the Interior region, and (D) microsatellite data generated from the Interior region. Dashed lines on each plot indicate average inter-individual genetic distances observed among all individuals in each dataset. Points marked with asterisks indicate values that are significantly larger or smaller than random expectations at the $\alpha = 0.05$ level. Cases where significant results are observed at the shortest class likely represent true significant spatial structure (Epperson, 2005).

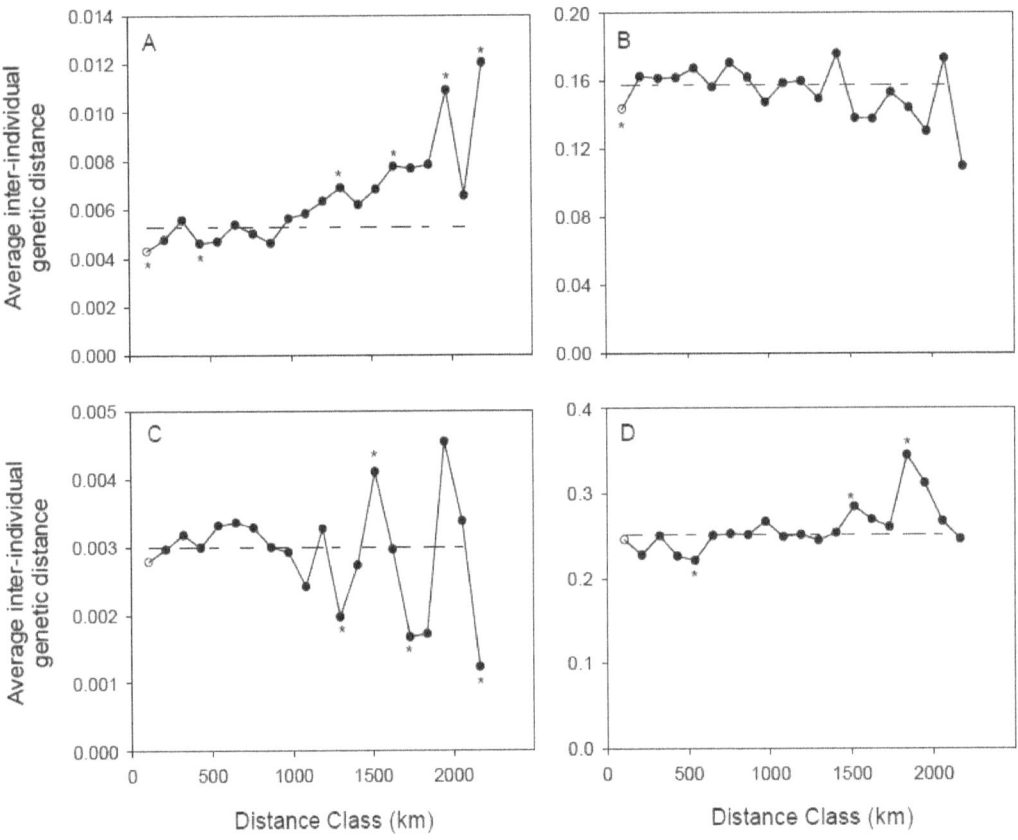

Figure 6. STRUCTURE analysis of microsatellite data for Piping Plovers. Panel A: Evaluation of 10 replicate runs for values of K ranging from 1-8 suggested that the $K = 2$ solution (two separate genetic clusters) was the most likely solution. Panel B: Individual cluster membership coefficients suggested that genetic structure was strongly divided between the Interior and Atlantic groups.

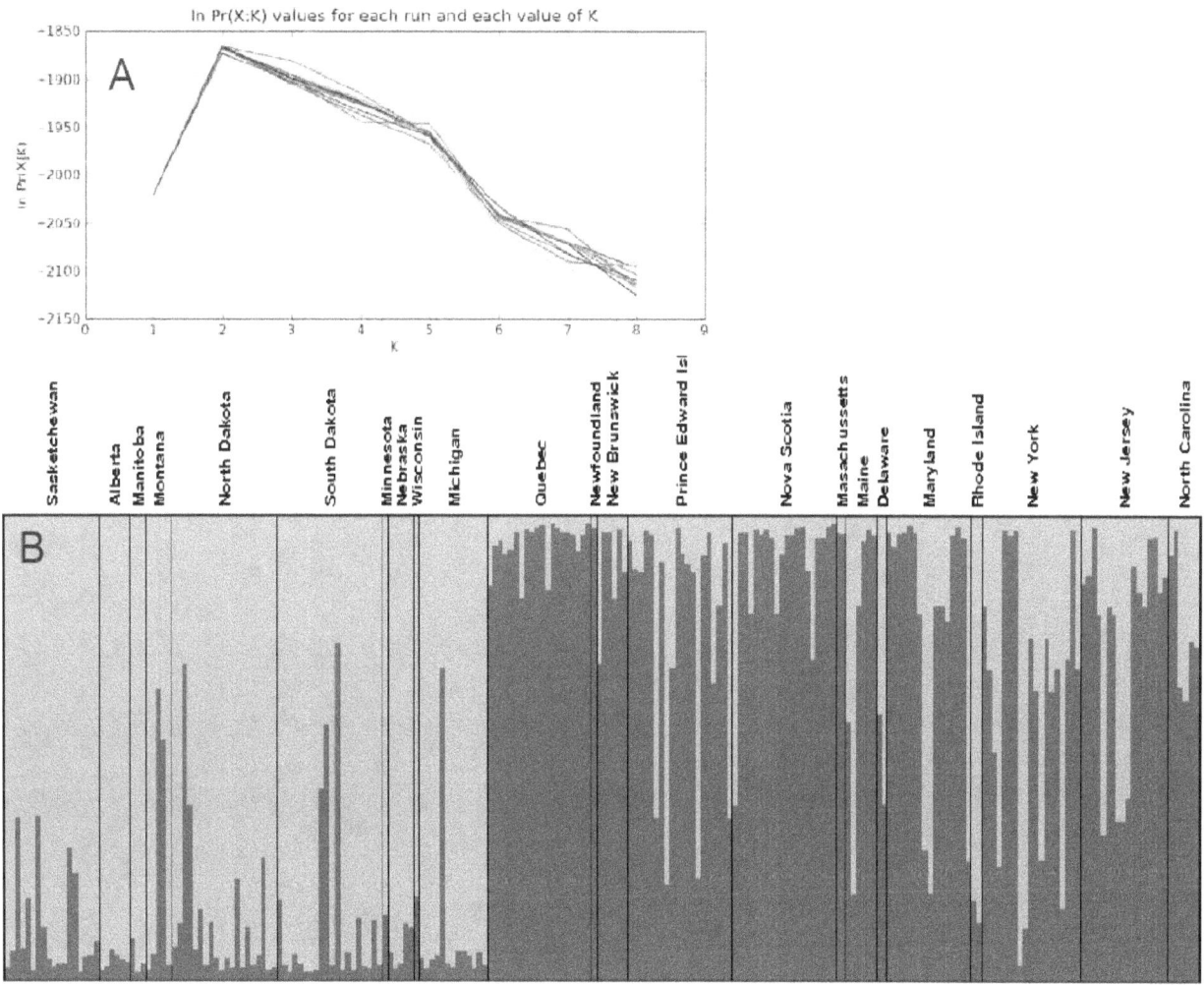

Appendix 1. Collection Years and U.S. State or Canadian Province of Each Piping Plover Used in Mitochondrial or Microsatellite Analyses. Collection years are unknown for 15 specimens included here but are less than 20 years old.

Genetic sample ID	Mitochondrial data	Microsatellite data	Year Collected	State or Province
SK1	y	y	1997	Saskatchewan
SK2	y	y	1997	Saskatchewan
SK3	y	y	1997	Saskatchewan
SK4	y	y	1997	Saskatchewan
SK5	y	n	2002	Saskatchewan
SK6	y	y	2002	Saskatchewan
SK7	y	y	2002	Saskatchewan
SK8	y	y	2002	Saskatchewan
SK9	y	y	2002	Saskatchewan
SK10	y	y	2002	Saskatchewan
SK11	y	y	2002	Saskatchewan
SK12	y	y	2002	Saskatchewan
SK13	y	y	2002	Saskatchewan
SK14	y	y	2002	Saskatchewan
SK15	y	y	2002	Saskatchewan
SK16	y	y	2001	Saskatchewan
SK17	y	y	2002	Saskatchewan
SK18	y	y	2002	Saskatchewan
SK19	y	y	2002	Saskatchewan
AB1	y	y	2001	Alberta
AB2	y	y	2001	Alberta
AB3	y	y	2001	Alberta
AB4	y	y	2001	Alberta
AB5	y	n	2001	Alberta
AB6	y	y	2001	Alberta
AB7	y	y	2001	Alberta
MB1	y	y	1999	Manitoba
MB2	y	y	2000	Manitoba
MB3	y	y	2000	Manitoba
MT1	y	y	1995	Montana
MT2	y	y	1995	Montana
MT3	y	y	1995	Montana
MT4	y	y	2008	Montana
MT5	y	y	2008	Montana
NE1	y	y	-	Nebraska
NE2	y	y	-	Nebraska
NE3	y	y	-	Nebraska
NE4	y	y	1996	Nebraska
NE5	y	y	-	Nebraska
NE19	y	n	1996	Nebraska

ND1	y	y	1995	North Dakota
ND2	y	y	1994	North Dakota
ND3	y	y	1992	North Dakota
ND4	y	y	1993	North Dakota
ND5	y	y	1995	North Dakota
ND6	y	y	1995	North Dakota
ND7	y	y	1995	North Dakota
ND8	y	y	1995	North Dakota
ND9	y	y	1995	North Dakota
ND10	y	y	1995	North Dakota
ND11	y	y	1995	North Dakota
ND12	y	y	1995	North Dakota
ND13	y	y	1996	North Dakota
ND14	y	y	1995	North Dakota
ND15	y	y	1995	North Dakota
ND16	y	y	1995	North Dakota
ND17	y	y	1995	North Dakota
ND18	y	y	1995	North Dakota
ND19	y	y	1995	North Dakota
ND20	y	y	1995	North Dakota
SD1	y	n	1993	South Dakota
SD2	y	y	1988	South Dakota
SD3	y	n	1988	South Dakota
SD4	y	y	1988	South Dakota
SD5	y	y	1988	South Dakota
SD6	y	y	1988	South Dakota
SD7	y	y	-	South Dakota
SD8	y	y	1995	South Dakota
SD9	y	y	1995	South Dakota
SD10	y	n	1995	South Dakota
SD11	y	n	1995	South Dakota
SD12	y	y	1995	South Dakota
SD13	y	n	1995	South Dakota
SD14	y	n	1995	South Dakota
SD15	y	n	1995	South Dakota
SD16	y	n	1995	South Dakota
SD17	y	y	1996	South Dakota
SD18	y	y	-	South Dakota
SD19	n	y	-	South Dakota
SD20	y	y	1996	South Dakota
SD21	n	y	1994	South Dakota
SD22	n	y	1994	South Dakota
SD23	n	y	1994	South Dakota
SD24	n	y	1994	South Dakota
SD25	n	y	1994	South Dakota
SD26	n	y	1994	South Dakota
SD27	n	y	1994	South Dakota
SD28	n	y	1994	South Dakota

MN1	y	y	1994	Minnesota
WI1	y	y	2001	Wisconsin
MI1	y	n	1991	Michigan
MI2	y	y	1993	Michigan
MI3	y	y	1993	Michigan
MI4	y	y	1994	Michigan
MI5	y	y	-	Michigan
MI6	y	y	1999	Michigan
MI7	y	y	1999	Michigan
MI8	y	n	1999	Michigan
MI9	y	y	1992	Michigan
MI10	y	y	-	Michigan
MI11	y	y	-	Michigan
MI12	y	y	-	Michigan
MI13	y	y	1994	Michigan
MI14	y	n	1992	Michigan
MI15	y	y	1992	Michigan
MI16	y	y	2001	Michigan
NS1	y	y	2001	Nova Scotia
NS2	y	y	2002	Nova Scotia
NS3	y	y	2002	Nova Scotia
NS4	y	n	2003	Nova Scotia
NS5	y	y	2003	Nova Scotia
NS6	y	y	2000	Nova Scotia
NS7	y	n	2001	Nova Scotia
NS8	y	n	2004	Nova Scotia
NS9	y	y	2000	Nova Scotia
NS10	y	y	2002	Nova Scotia
NS11	y	y	2002	Nova Scotia
NS12	y	y	2002	Nova Scotia
NS13	y	n	2003	Nova Scotia
NS14	y	y	2000	Nova Scotia
NS15	y	y	2003	Nova Scotia
NS16	y	y	2003	Nova Scotia
NS17	y	y	2004	Nova Scotia
NS18	y	y	2004	Nova Scotia
NS19	y	y	2003	Nova Scotia
NS20	y	y	2003	Nova Scotia
NS21	y	y	2004	Nova Scotia
NS22	n	y	2004	Nova Scotia
NS23	n	y	2004	Nova Scotia
NS26	n	y	2004	Nova Scotia
NF1	y	n	2004	Newfoundland
NF2	y	y	2000	Newfoundland
NB1	y	y	2001	New Brunswick
NB2	y	y	2003	New Brunswick
NB3	y	y	2004	New Brunswick

NB4	y	y	2004	New Brunswick
NB5	y	y	2004	New Brunswick
NB6	y	y	2004	New Brunswick
PEI1	y	y	1994	Prince Edward Island
PEI2	y	y	1994	Prince Edward Island
PEI3	y	y	1994	Prince Edward Island
PEI4	y	y	1994	Prince Edward Island
PEI5	y	y	1994	Prince Edward Island
PEI6	y	y	1995	Prince Edward Island
PEI7	y	y	1994	Prince Edward Island
PEI8	y	y	1994	Prince Edward Island
PEI9	y	y	1994	Prince Edward Island
PEI10	y	y	1995	Prince Edward Island
PEI11	y	y	1994	Prince Edward Island
PEI12	y	y	1995	Prince Edward Island
PEI13	y	y	1994	Prince Edward Island
PEI14	y	y	1995	Prince Edward Island
PEI15	y	y	1994	Prince Edward Island
PEI16	y	y	1995	Prince Edward Island
PEI17	y	y	1994	Prince Edward Island
PEI18	y	y	1994	Prince Edward Island
PEI19	y	y	1994	Prince Edward Island
PEI20	y	y	2005	Prince Edward Island
QB1	y	y	1995	Quebec
QB2	y	y	1995	Quebec
QB3	y	y	1995	Quebec
QB4	y	y	1995	Quebec
QB5	y	y	1995	Quebec
QB6	y	y	1995	Quebec
QB7	y	y	1995	Quebec
QB8	y	y	1995	Quebec
QB9	y	y	1995	Quebec
QB10	y	y	2006	Quebec
QB11	y	y	2005	Quebec
QB12	y	y	2005	Quebec
QB13	y	n	2004	Quebec
QB14	y	y	2004	Quebec
QB15	y	y	2004	Quebec
QB16	y	y	2003	Quebec
QB17	y	y	2001	Quebec
QB18	y	y	2001	Quebec
QB19	y	y	2000	Quebec
QB20	y	y	1999	Quebec
QC21	n	y	2001	Quebec
ME1	y	n	1994	Maine
ME2	y	y	1999	Maine
ME3	y	y	1999	Maine
ME4	y	y	1996	Maine
ME5	y	y	-	Maine

ME6	y	y	-	Maine
ME7	n	y	-	Maine
MA1	y	y	1999	Massachusetts
MA2	n	y	-	Massachusetts
DE1	y	y	1996	Delaware
DE2	y	y	1996	Delaware
MD1	y	y	1995	Maryland
MD2	y	y	1994	Maryland
MD3	y	y	1994	Maryland
MD4	y	y	1994	Maryland
MD5	y	y	1994	Maryland
MD6	y	y	1994	Maryland
MD7	y	y	1997	Maryland
MD8	y	y	1997	Maryland
MD9	y	y	1996	Maryland
MD10	y	y	1998	Maryland
MD11	y	y	1998	Maryland
MD12	y	y	1998	Maryland
MD13	y	y	1998	Maryland
MD14	y	y	1996	Maryland
MD15	y	y	1996	Maryland
MD16	y	y	1996	Maryland
MD17	y	n	1996	Maryland
RI1	y	y	1995	Rhode Island
RI2	y	y	1995	Rhode Island
RI3	y	n	1995	Rhode Island
NY1	y	y	1996	New York
NY2	y	y	1996	New York
NY3	y	y	1996	New York
NY4	y	y	1996	New York
NY5	y	y	1996	New York
NY6	y	y	1996	New York
NY7	y	y	1996	New York
NY8	y	y	1997	New York
NY9	y	y	1997	New York
NY10	y	y	1997	New York
NY11	y	y	1997	New York
NY12	y	y	1997	New York
NY13	y	y	1997	New York
NY14	y	n	1997	New York
NY15	y	y	1997	New York
NY16	y	y	1997	New York
NY17	y	y	1997	New York
NY18	y	y	1997	New York
NY19	y	n	1997	New York
NY20	y	y	1997	New York
NY21	n	y	1997	New York

NJ1	y	y	1995	New Jersey
NJ2	y	y	1995	New Jersey
NJ3	y	y	1995	New Jersey
NJ4	y	y	1995	New Jersey
NJ5	y	y	1995	New Jersey
NJ6	y	y	1995	New Jersey
NJ7	y	y	1995	New Jersey
NJ8	y	y	1996	New Jersey
NJ9	y	y	1992	New Jersey
NJ10	y	y	1992	New Jersey
NJ11	y	y	1992	New Jersey
NJ12	y	y	1992	New Jersey
NJ13	y	n	1994	New Jersey
NJ14	y	y	1995	New Jersey
NJ15	y	y	1995	New Jersey
NJ16	y	y	1995	New Jersey
NJ17	y	y	1991	New Jersey
NJ18	y	y	1992	New Jersey
NJ19	y	n	1995	New Jersey
NJ20	y	n	1996	New Jersey
NJ21	y	n	1996	New Jersey
NJ22	y	n	1997	New Jersey
NC1	y	y	1995	North Carolina
NC2	y	y	1995	North Carolina
NC3	y	n	1994	North Carolina
NC4	y	y	1995	North Carolina
NC5	y	y	1995	North Carolina
NC6	y	y	1995	North Carolina
NC7	y	n	1995	North Carolina
NC8	y	n	1995	North Carolina
NC9	y	y	1996	North Carolina